I0025536

Demography and the development potential of sub-Saharan Africa

Bo Malmberg

NORDISKA AFRIKAINSTITUTET, UPPSALA 2008

A background paper commissioned by the Nordic Africa Institute
for the Swedish Government White Paper on Africa.

INDEXING TERMS:
Demography
Demographic transition
Demographic change
Population growth
Development potential
Economic and social development
Demographic analysis
Demographic statistics
Africa south of Sahara

The opinions expressed in this volume are those of the author
and do not necessarily reflect the views of the Nordic Africa Institute.

Language checking: Peter Colenbrander
ISSN 0280-2171
ISBN 978-91-7106-621-3 (print)
ISBN 978-91-7106-629-9 (electronic)
© The author and Nordiska Afrikainstitutet 2008
Printed in Sweden by Elanders Sverige AB, Mölnlycke 2008
Grafisk form Elin Olsson, Today Press AB

CONTENTS

List of Figures

List of Tables

List of acronyms

HIV	Human Immunodeficiency Virus
UN	United Nations
TFR	Total Fertility Rate
IMR	Infant Mortality Rate
IMF	International Monetary Fund
TB	Tuberculosis

Executive Summary

This is one of five background papers for the White Paper on Africa that the Swedish government will submit to parliament in early 2008. It presents historical and future demographic trends in sub-Saharan African and relates them to the social and economic trends in the sub-continent. The main analytical tool is the current theory of the demographic transition and there is an emphasis on comparing sub-Saharan Africa's development to trends in other parts of the world.

There are three main conclusions.

1. Sub-Saharan Africa is currently about halfway through the transition from high to low death and birth rates. A mid-20th century reduction in death rates has generated a period of rapid population increase. Only in the last 25 years have there been clear signs of declining fertility and the decline has been slow and has at times stalled.

2. Many of the socioeconomic trends that have characterised sub-Saharan Africa during the last decades (stagnating per capita income, high poverty rates, environmental degradation, current account deficits, widespread use of child labour, violent internal conflicts, rapid urbanisation and increasing migration flows) are typical of countries that are in a phase of rapid population growth, high rates of child dependency and a rapidly increasing young adult population. If sub-Saharan Africa succeeds in completing the demographic transition by establishing low fertility rates and further reductions in mortality, this is likely to generate the same type of positive economic effect that has been seen in East Asia, India and Latin America.

3. Efficient policies that promote health, increases in education and improvements in infrastructure can be pivotal for a shift towards more favourable demographic trends. The AIDS epidemic is devastating, but probably possible to control provided appropriate measures are pursued vigorously.

Bo Malmberg

1.Purpose and outline

Both popular and scholarly views on population are often influenced by strong and some-
times mistaken preconceptions. Views concerning the population trends in sub-Saharan Africa are no exception. Here, a standard view would be that sub-Saharan Africa is burdened
by high rates of population growth flowing from high fertility rates. High population growth
rates have led to widespread poverty and environmental degradation and, more recently, to
an increase in outward migration. In addition, with the advent of the HIV epidemic, this
population is now threatened by a mortality crisis. This description of the demographic
situation in sub-Saharan Africa is not entirely incorrect. However, to describe sub-Saharan
Africa is this way implies that the sub-continent is represented as a typical case of Malthusian
development, and such a description is not politically innocent. For example, it indirectly
implies that the development problems of sub-Saharan Africa are caused by a population
that is too large. Moreover, in the Malthusian story, increasing mortality is seen as a result
of, and possibly a remedy for, over-population. Likewise, outward migration is depicted as a
desperate attempt to escape from an intolerable situation.

The main conclusion of the analysis presented below is that a Malthusian interpretation
leads to a mistaken view of the role that population plays, and will play, in the development
of sub-Saharan Africa. Instead, it is more fruitful to analyse population change in sub-Saharan Africa as a recent example of the kind of developments that characterise a region that
undergoes a *demographic transition* from high death and birth rates to low death and birth
rates. One advantage of adopting this perspective is that it will show that the current situation in sub-Saharan Africa is not a unique event that lacks precedents in the recent history
of Europe, Asia and America. On the contrary, developments in sub-Saharan Africa are in
many ways similar to what has been observed earlier in countries that have experienced similar demographic trends. Another advantage of the transition perspective is that it not only
allows an understanding of current trends in relation to similar event in other regions, it also
allows for rational speculation on what the future trends in sub-Saharan Africa will be and
how these can be influenced by policies.

Section 2 presents the demographic transition, the basic concept used to analyse the
development of sub-Saharan Africa. Sections 3, 4 and 5 discuss the main driving forces
behind the demographic transition, infant mortality, life expectancy and fertility. Section 5
and section 6 discuss the effect of the demographic transition on population growth and age
structure, and how population growth and age-structure change have affected sub-Saharan
Africa's social and economic trends. Sections 8, 9 and 10 provide a more detailed discussion
of the effects of demographic change, and in section 11 this discussion is summarised in the
outlining of a possible future scenario for sub-Saharan Africa. The conclusion is laid out in
Section 12.

2.The demographic transition

The demographic transition is the process whereby a country moves from a demographic regime with high mortality and high fertility to a regime characterised by low mortality and low
fertility (see Figure 1). The demographic transition was first observed during the interwar
years in 19th and 20th century demographic data for Northern and Western Europe. In the
mid-1940s, a group of demographers at Princeton University proposed that the same pattern
of mortality and fertility decline that had been observed in the Western world would, in the
postwar period, also be observed in the rest of the world. This turned out to be perhaps the
best prediction made by social scientists in the 20th century (Davis 1945; Notestein 1945).

FIGURE 1. THE DEMOGRAPHIC TRANSITION

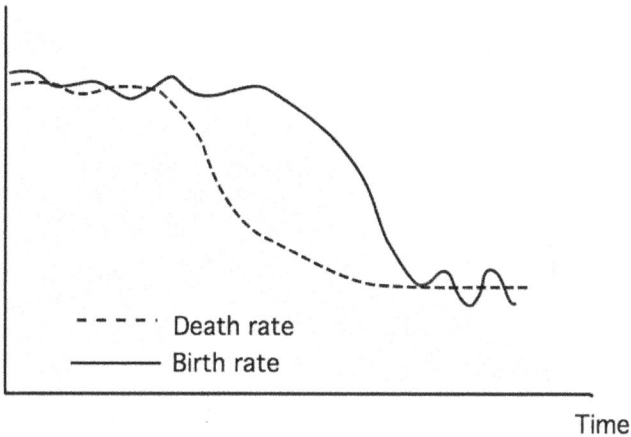

By the 1960s, substantial declines in mortality had been achieved in almost all developing
countries, but fertility rates were still high. The results were rapid population growth and
some leading scholars claimed that the world was heading towards a catastrophe. A delay in
the fertility decline was, however, in line with the experience of Western countries, where
declines in mortality predated the fertility decline. And in the 1970s, 1980s and 1990s the
Princeton prediction turned out to be correct as fertility rates started to come down in a wide
range of countries in Asia, Latin America and Northern Africa (see Figure 2).

Sub-Saharan Africa has also been a part of this process. Due to lack of data it is difficult
to pinpoint when the mortality rates in sub-Saharan Africa started to decline. Some sources
suggest that there was an improvement in the interwar years, but it could be the case that it
was only after 1945 that a more general trend towards lower mortality was established. This
is, for example, what the UN post-1950 data suggest. A significant post-1945 downturn is
also likely, given the rapid diffusion of DDT spraying during this period.

Irrespective of when the downward trend started, it is, however, clear that by the
early 1950s sub-Saharan Africa had entered into the mortality decline phase of the demographic transition. From 1950-55, the death rate in sub-Saharan Africa was down to
27 per thousand. Given a birth rate of 49 per thousand, this generates a rate of natural

FIGURE 2. THE DEMOGRAPHIC TRANSITION IN LESS DEVELOPED REGIONS, EXCLUDING CHINA

(UNITED NATIONS. POPULATION DIVISION 2007)

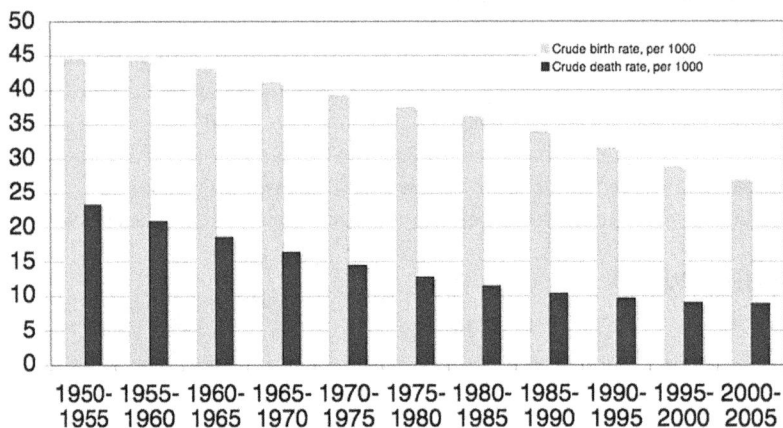

population growth of 2.2%, which is high by historical standards. The downward trend in death rates continued, and with birth rates relatively stable, the result was a further acceleration in population growth. According to the UN, the rate of population growth reached its maximum in 1980-85, at 3.0% growth per year.

For decades, the progress of the mortality decline was relatively uniform across the regions of sub-Saharan Africa. The United Nations divides sub-Saharan Africa into four regions: Western Africa, Central Africa, Eastern Africa and Southern Africa. Of these regions, Western and Eastern Africa have about 75% of the total sub-Saharan Africa population. Southern Africa has less than 10% of the population and Middle Africa about 15%. Of these regions, Southern Africa has been leading the decline in infant mortality. Here, the infant mortality had already fallen below 100 deaths in the first year of life per thousand births in the late 1950s at a time when the other regions had an IMR close to 200. In the early 1990s, when infant mortality in the rest of sub-Saharan Africa was still over 100, it was down to 50 in Southern Africa. A possible reason for the earlier mortality decline in this region is a more developed economy. However, public health measures should not be disregarded. The anti-malaria campaigns in Southern Africa seem to have been pursued with more determination than in other regions of sub-Saharan Africa, possibly because of the presence of a large white population. In fact, it has been suggested that apartheid was first conceived as a policy aimed at protecting the white population from malaria infection.

Sub-Saharan Africa has thus participated in the downward trend in mortality. However, for the entire postwar period, the mortality situation in sub-Saharan Africa has been worse than in other developing countries. The gap vis-à-vis Asia was relatively small in 1950 but has widened more and more with each decade, and especially after 1990, when AIDS-mortality increased.

The second phase of the demographic transition begins when fertility starts to decline. In sub-Saharan Africa this happened around 1980. At that time, African women,

FIGURE 3. TOTAL FERTILITY RATE BY WORLD REGIONS 1950-2005

(UNITED NATIONS. POPULATION DIVISION 2007)

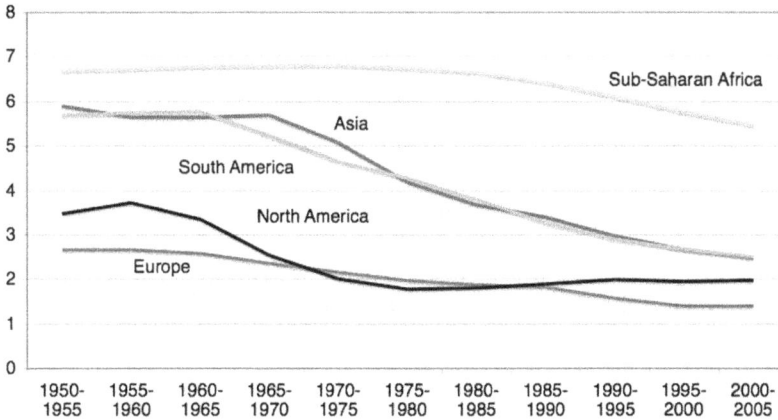

on average, gave birth to seven children during their fertile years. Since then, the total fertility rate has fallen by 25%. But, given the high level when the decline began, fertility is still very high. Sub-Saharan women now, on average, give birth to 5.1 children. This is higher than the fertility rate was in Sweden in the 19th century before the decline started. As seen in Figure 3, the fertility decline in sub-Saharan Africa lags considerably behind Asia and South America.

The length of the mortality and fertility lag is about 40 years. Looking at the figures above, it can be seen that the infant mortality rate in sub-Saharan Africa today is at the same level as in Asia in the early 1970s. Fertility is at about the same level as it was in Asia and South America around 1970. Thus, if sub-Saharan Africa were able to follow the same demographic trajectory as Asia, infant mortality could be approaching 50 deaths per thousand and the total fertility rate could approach two children per women. Since this is a development path that has been followed by a large region starting from a similar demographic situation, it cannot be ruled out as a possibility for sub-Saharan Africa. But how probable is a scenario of this sort? Isn't sub-Saharan Africa inherently different in a way that makes it unlikely that the sub-continent will follow a demographic trajectory that is similar to, for example, Asia?

One way to answer this question is to analyse whether the demographic trends in sub-Saharan Africa, and the socioeconomic effects of demographic change, deviate from what one should expect from comparisons with development trajectories in other parts of the world.

9

Bo Malmberg

3. Infant mortality

The level of mortality in a population can be measured by the crude death rate (number of deaths per thousand inhabitants), the infant mortality rate (number of infant deaths per thousand births) and life expectancy (a summary measure of death risks/ survival chances over different ages). Of these, the infant mortality rate is the most widely used indicator of the general health situation in a country.

In Figure 4, the development of the infant mortality rate from 1950-2010 for sub-Saharan Africa is compared with the trend in infant mortality in other parts of the world. What is evident from this graph is that the improvements in child health in sub-Saharan Africa have been slower than in other parts of the world. In the 1950s, infant mortality rates in Asia were as high as in sub-Saharan Africa, but after 1960, the decline became more rapid in Asia, whereas the decline in sub-Saharan Africa continued at a slow pace.

FIGURE 4. INFANT MORTALITY IN WORLD REGIONS 1950-2005
(UNITED NATIONS. POPULATION DIVISION 2007)

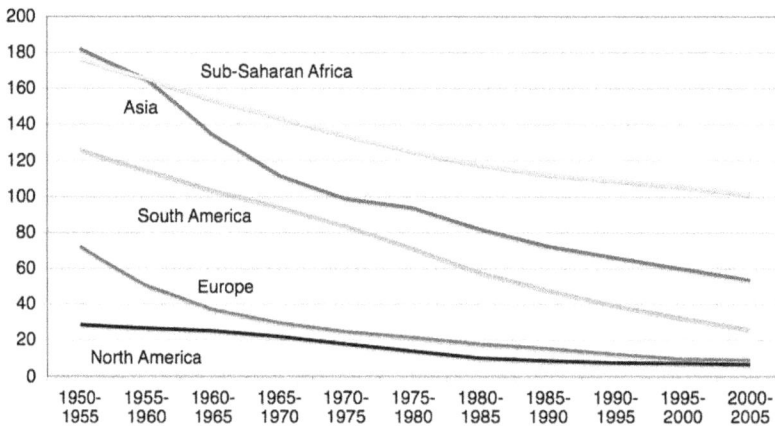

Within this general trend, there have been differences among the experiences of individual countries. In about half of the sub-Saharan African countries, the decline in the infant mortality rate has been more or less continuous (see map below). Infant mortality rates in this group were above 150 per thousand births in the early 1950s, but have now declined to under 100. In the remaining countries, the decline in infant mortality was relatively rapid until the 1980s, but then the downward trend was broken. In some countries, this levelling off of the decline came when the infant mortality rate had fallen below 100. In others, the stall meant the infant mortality rate remained at a level above 100 (see map below).

Figure 5 shows the average rate of decline across the sub-Saharan African countries from 1950-2005. From this graph it is clear that the improvements in infant survival accelerated in the late 1960s and then slowed in the 1980s with a near halt around the Millennium. However, according to the UN, the rate of improvement has picked up in recent years, implying a return to rates of decline that are comparable to the level in the 1970s.

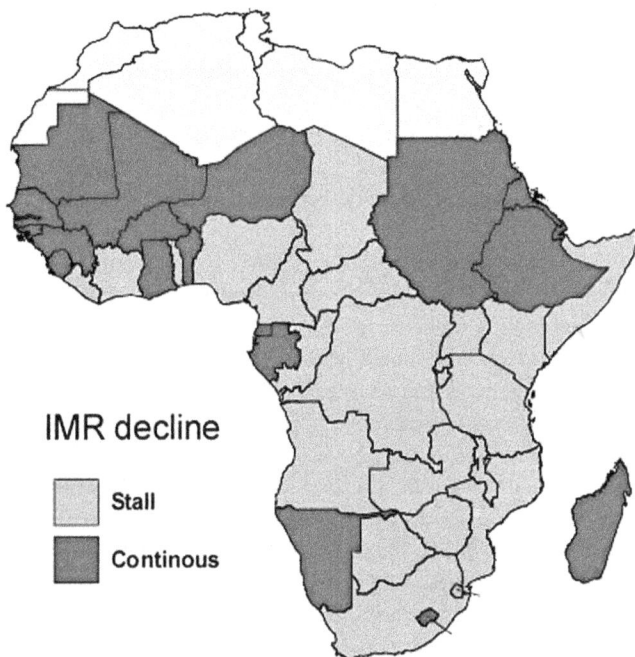

IMR decline

Stall

Continous

FIGURE 5. ANNUAL DECLINE IN INFANT MORTALITY RATE, SUB-SAHARAN AFRICA, 1950-2010

(UNITED NATIONS. POPULATION DIVISION 2007)

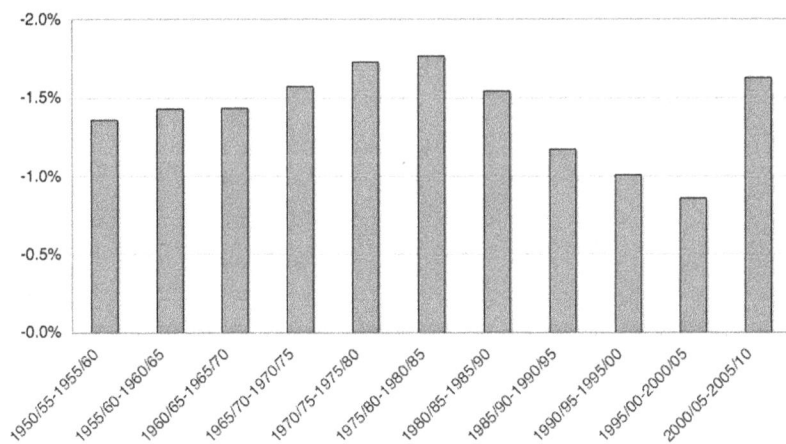

The stall in the infant mortality rate decline during the last two decades of the 20th century can be seen as the result of a policy failure. One possible reason for low rates of improvement after 1980 could be the austerity measures imposed on many sub-Saharan countries by the IMF and the World Bank. Severe cuts in government budgets and large lay-offs of public employees seem to have had negative effects on programmes aimed at health improvement. An alternative explanation is that the economic downturn was the key factor. What is clear is that sub-Saharan Africa during this period was unable to implement the kinds of broad-based health policies that have been so successful in reducing infant-mortality in Asia (Fort, Mercer et al. 2004).

Hopefully, the stall in the mortality decline will prove to have been temporary. The negative mortality consequences of the austerity policy have stimulated a rethinking in the World Bank and there is now much more emphasis on health improvements in the international discussion. If the new turn-around envisioned by the UN materialises and sub-Saharan Africa comes back on the demographic transition track, this would constitute an important demonstration that the international community can both formulate and implement policies that improve the living conditions for broad groups of people.

Furthermore, the kind of setback that sub-Saharan Africa suffered during the closing years of the 20th century is not unique. A similar increase in mortality affected England (Huck 1995) and the United States during the 19th century (Haines and Steckel 2000). Mortality increased as a consequence of rapid urbanisation and poor health conditions in urban areas. Large reductions in infant mortality in these countries didn't start until the end of the 19th century, and then in response to ambitious efforts to improve public health (Cain and Rotella 2001).

4. Life expectancy

Infant mortality is an important aggregate measure of the health situation in a country. It does not, however, capture changes in adult mortality. An alternative measure that accounts for death risks over the entire lifespan is life expectancy at birth. The trend in this measure for sub-Saharan Africa is displayed in Figure 6.

FIGURE 6. LIFE EXPECTANCY AT BIRTH BY WORLD REGIONS
(UNITED NATIONS. POPULATION DIVISION 2007)

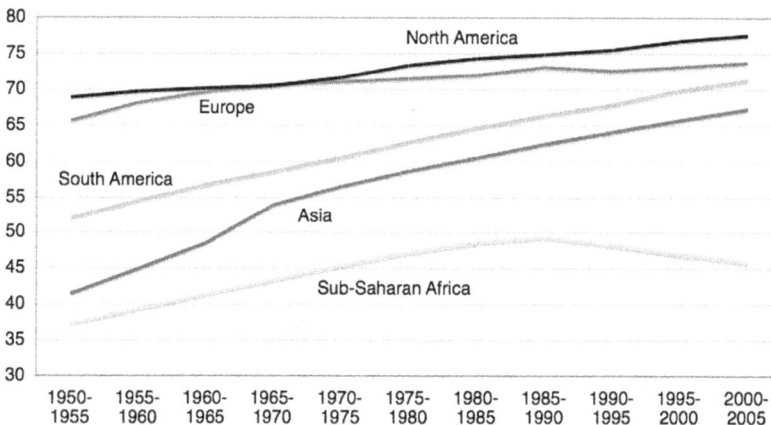

As can be seen in Figure 6, life expectancy increased in sub-Saharan Africa until the late 1980s. After 1990, however, life expectancy has declined. The main reason for this decline is the AIDS epidemic (United Nations. Population Division 2006).

The area hardest hit by the epidemic is Southern Africa, as can be seen from Figure 7 and Figure 8. In Zimbawe, Botswana, Swaziland, Lesotho, Zambia, South Africa and Namibia, life expectancy declined by 10-22 years, according to the latest estimates from the United Nations Population Division (2006 revision). It should be noted that these estimates, except for Zimbabwe, are much lower than those presented in the 2004 revision.

The second hardest hit area is Eastern and Central Africa: Uganda, Tanzania, Burundi, Malawi, Cameroon, Congo, Dem. Republic of Congo, Central African Republic. Here, life expectancy declined by 4-8 years from a peak value before 1995.

In other parts of sub-Saharan Africa, the AIDS epidemic has not given rise to a de facto decline in life expectancy.

The geographical patterns of changes in life expectancy can be seen to reflect the spread of the epidemic since the late 1970s. The first countries to be affected by declining life expectancy were in Central Africa and in neighbouring countries: Congo, Dem. Republic of Congo, Central African Republic, Zambia, Burundi and Uganda. The second group to be affected was further to the east and to the south: Kenya, Tanzania, Malawi, Zimbabwe, Botswana. Not until the late 1990s did life expectancy start to decline in South Africa, Namibia and Lesotho.

FIGURE 7. TRENDS IN LIFE EXPECTANCY FOR SELECTED SUB-SAHARAN COUNTRIES

(UNITED NATIONS. POPULATION DIVISION 2007)

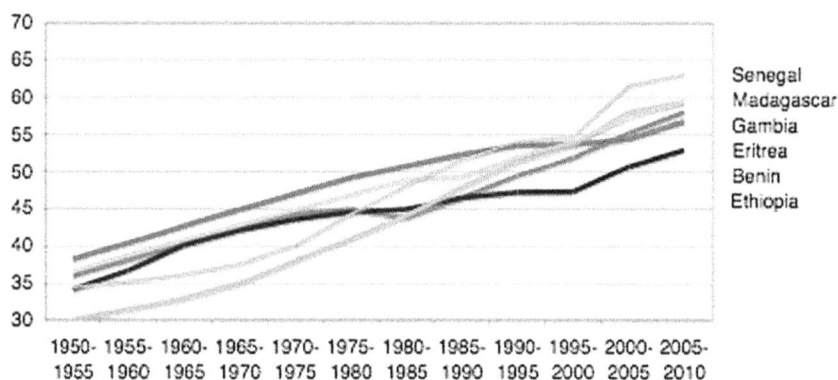

Senegal
Madagascar
Gambia
Eritrea
Benin
Ethiopia

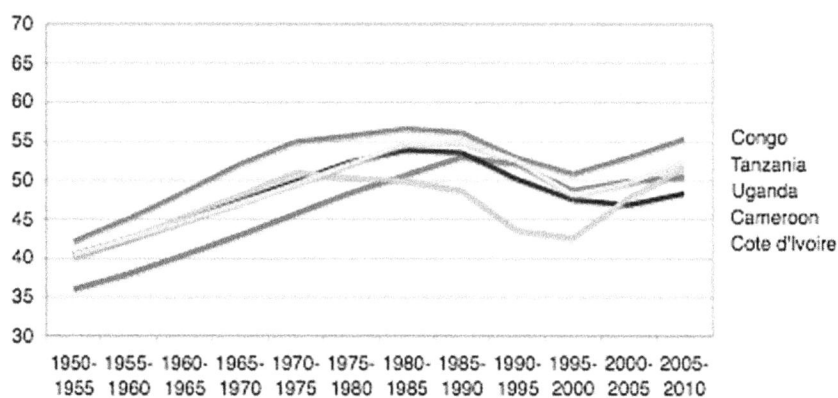

Congo
Tanzania
Uganda
Cameroon
Cote d'Ivoire

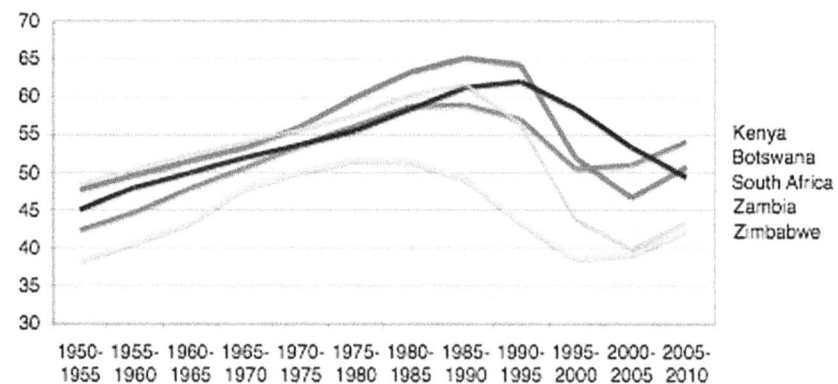

Kenya
Botswana
South Africa
Zambia
Zimbabwe

FIGURE 8. HIV PREVALENCE IN SUB-SAHARAN AFRICA

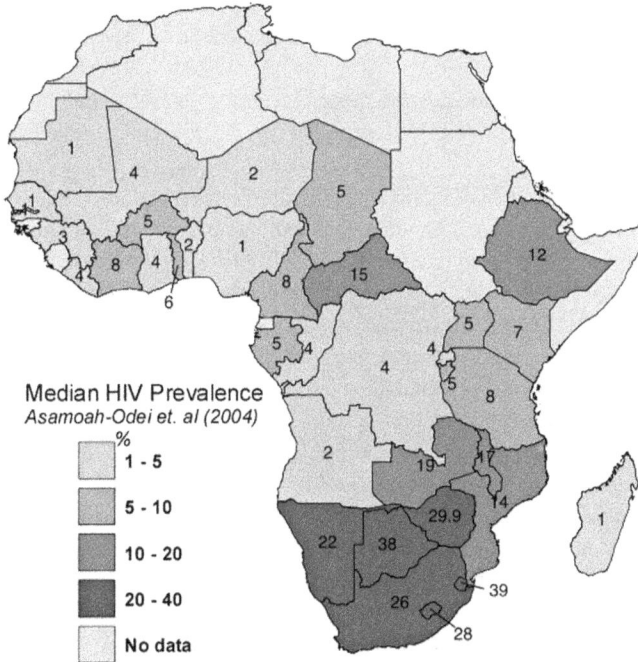

Median HIV Prevalence
Asamoah-Odei et. al (2004)
%
1 - 5
5 - 10
10 - 20
20 - 40
No data

An important feature in the latest UN estimates is that in most of the countries that experienced an early decline in life expectancy, there has now been a turn-around: life-expectancies are rising again. The most dramatic revision has been made for Botswana. In the 2004 revision, life expectancy in Botswana was estimated to be 36.6 years in 2000-05, and 33.9 years in 2005-10, down from 65.1 years in 1985-90. In the 2006 revision, published in March 2007, the 2000-05 estimate is 46.6 years and the 2005-10 estimate 50.7 years. This new estimate reduces the decline in life expectancy between 1985-90 and 2005-10 from 31.2 years to 14.4 years. A 14.4 year decline in life expectancy is still a huge drop, but a life expectancy of 51 years provides much better prospects for social and economic development than a life expectancy of 34 years.

According to the new estimates, the AIDS catastrophe should not be seen as a generalised phenomenon in sub-Saharan Africa, but rather as a regional disaster. Alongside Botswana, countries where life expectancy is 10 years lower than the peak level include South Africa, Swaziland, Lesotho and Zimbabwe, and no other. Life expectancy is below its peak level in 10 more countries, but for the majority of sub-Saharan countries, life expectancy today is, according to the UN, at its highest level ever.

Three factors are responsible for the upward revisions of life expectancy estimates. First, there has been a downward revision of the HIV prevalence rates based on new nationally representative data. Second, in many countries HIV prevalence rates are no longer increasing and in some there are even declines. Third, the UN now takes into account the fact that a substantial part of the HIV-affected population have, or will have, access to antiretroviral treatment.

Thus, currently, despair is not the most adequate reaction to the HIV epidemic. Rather, it seems that this is an epidemic that could be controlled given a continued and even stepped-up commitment to the task.

With these developments, the HIV epidemic has begun to take on a form that is recognisable from earlier epidemics that have threatened the health of human populations. European examples include the 1350-1710 plague epidemic, the 1490-1900 epidemic of syphilis and the 1750-1950 epidemic of tuberculosis. All three of these epidemics were eventually curbed by a combination of social control measures, behavioural change and medication. Perhaps the tuberculosis epidemic is of most relevance to the HIV epidemic. Tuberculosis became an increasing problem at a time when there had been considerable successes in combating other infectious diseases. It was a disease that increased adult mortality and it was chronic. Treating TB was costly and complicated, and progress in reducing TB mortality required large social investments. Thus, it isn't improbable that successful control of the HIV epidemic will require a broad-based approach similar to the one set in place in Europe and the United States to combat TB. On the other hand, the TB experience shows that success is possible, and the TB campaign can serve as a source of inspiration. A number of well-known European authors started their careers as patients in TB care facilities. Their subsequent work, which would not have appeared if they had succumbed, is therefore living evidence of the possible gains from the successful treatment of individuals with deadly diseases.

5. Fertility

With respect to current fertility, the sub-Saharan countries can be divided into four groups (see Figure 9).

A small group of countries in Southern Africa, among them South Africa, Zimbabwe, Botswana and Namibia, have come relatively far in the fertility transition. Here the total fertility rate is below 3.5 children per women.

FIGURE 9. TOTAL FERTILITY RATE IN SUB-SAHARAN AFRICA, 2005-2010

(UNITED NATIONS. POPULATION DIVISION 2007)

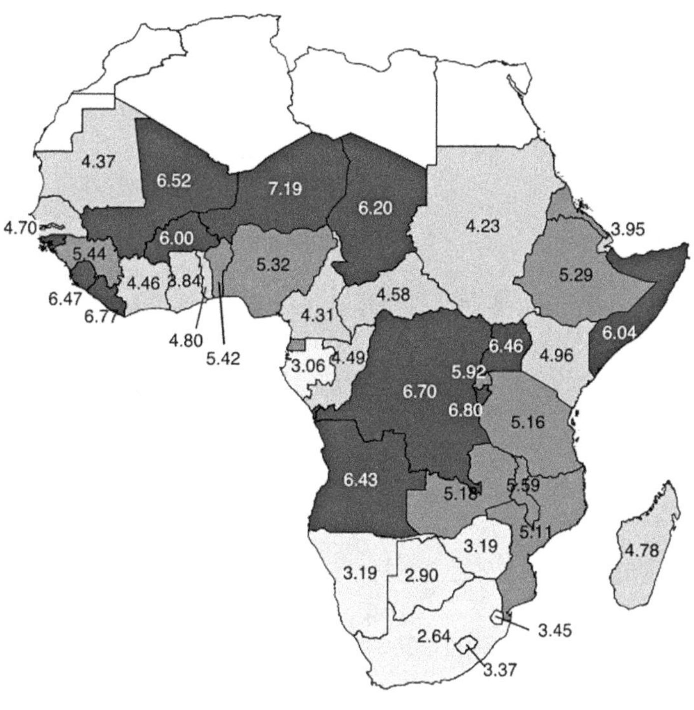

© Bo Malmberg, 2007

A second group, consisting of countries in both Eastern Africa (Kenya, Madagascar), Central Africa (Congo, Cameroon, Central African Republic), Western Africa (among them Ghana, Senegal, Côte d'Ivoire), and North-Eastern Africa (Djibouti, Sudan) have come relatively far in the fertility transition. They have now a total fertility rate below 5 children per woman.

A third group of countries – including Nigeria and a number of East African countries from Mozambique to Ethiopia and Eritrea – are in the early stages of the fertility transition. Here the fertility rates have fallen below six children per woman but TFR is still above five.

Finally, there is a group of countries were the fertility decline has only just started. This group consists of four Sahel countries (Mali, Burkina Faso, Niger and Chad), Guinea-Bissau and Sierra Leone in West Africa; Congo, Burundi and Uganda in Central Africa; plus Angola and Somalia. In these countries, the total fertility rate is still above six children per woman.

The most important determinant of these differences in fertility is the infant mortality rate. This is shown in Figure 10 below. For countries with an infant mortality rate above 100 dead infants per thousand births the typical fertility rate is around six or even higher. As infant mortality falls below 100, the fertility rate tends to decline below 6. And when infant mortality approaches 50, the total fertility rate can be expected to approach three children per woman.

FIGURE 10. CORRELATION BETWEEN INFANT MORTALITY AND FERTILITY, SUB-SAHARAN AFRICA 2000-05
(UNITED NATIONS. POPULATION DIVISION 2007)

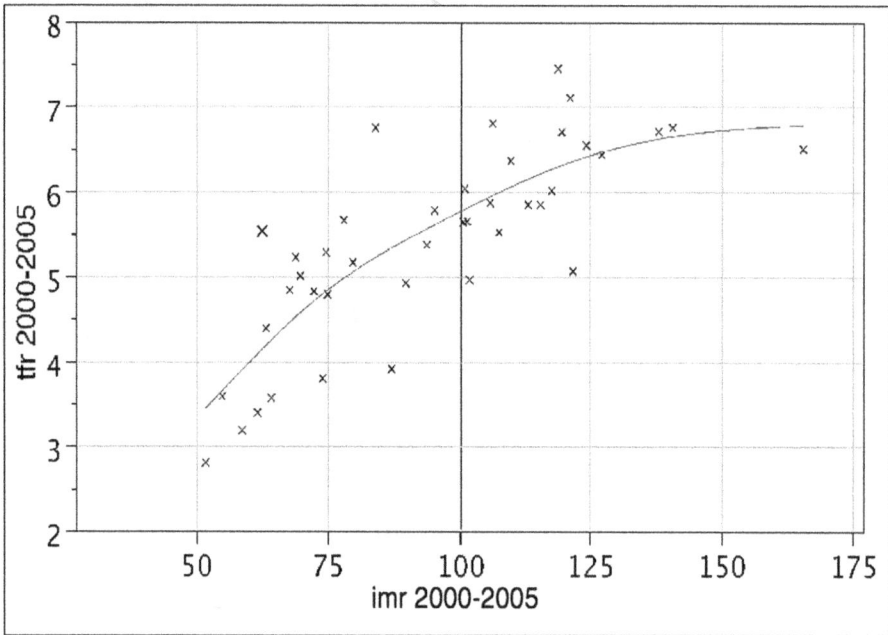

As discussed above, there was a stall in the decline in infant mortality in sub-Saharan Africa during the 1980s and 1990s. Considering the close correlation between infant mortality and fertility, it is likely that this stall has contributed to a slower fertility decline. Kenya and Tanzania provide two interesting examples. In both countries, fertility started to decline around 1980 after a 20 year period of declining infant mortality. The decline was faster in Kenya, were the reductions in infant mortality had been larger. In both countries, however, the decline in infant mortality levelled off in the late 1980s and this led to stagnation in the fertility decline also. The conclusion is that efforts to reduce infant mortality should be pursued more vigorously as a means to stimulate lower fertility.

6. Population growth

Decreasing infant mortality in combination with high fertility rates has given rise to rapid population growth in sub-Saharan Africa. In 2005, the population in sub-Saharan Africa was more than four times as large as in 1950. This implies that the population of sub-Saharan Africa today is larger than the population in Europe: 769 million inhabitants compared to 731 million in Europe. Fifty years ago, Europe's population was three times larger than the population in sub-Saharan Africa.

The population increase in sub-Saharan Africa during the last 50 years is equal in size to the population growth that Europe experienced between 1750 and 1950. In both cases, the population quadrupled: from 144 million to 543 million in Europe, and from 180 million to 769 million in sub-Saharan Africa.

Rapid population growth has had two important consequences: a radical transformation of sub-Saharan agriculture and the creation of a sub-Saharan urban system. The theory of how agriculture is influenced by population growth was developed by the Danish economist Esther Boserup (Boserup 1965; Boserup 1981). In essence, her theory states that population growth leads to increased intensification of agricultural production. Less intensive forms of agriculture are hunting and gathering, forest fallow, bush fallow agriculture, whereas short-fallow, annual cropping and multi-cropping are more intensive forms (in order of increasing intensity). Boserup's theory has stood up well to empirical testing, including in the African context. Thus, population growth has led to an expansion of more intensive forms of agriculture, with more land being used for cropping at the expense of forestry and herding. There has also been an expansion of new crops with high caloric yields per hectare, such as maize and cassava. A rapid mobilisation of natural resources for the purpose of food production has also had adverse effects such as erosion. Still, during the last 25 years, per capita food production has kept pace with the fast population increase (Food and Agriculture Organisation of the United Nations 2004).

Figure 11 and Figure 12 below show the population growth in sub-Saharan Africa divided into urban and rural growth. The figures demonstrate that the growth rate has been much higher

FIGURE 11. URBAN POPULATION GROWTH IN SUB-SAHARAN AFRICA

(MILLIONS, MEAN GROWTH RATE 4.7%)

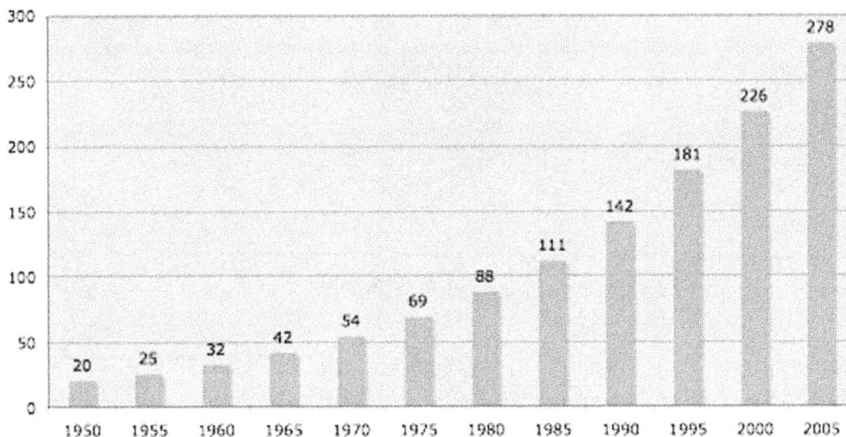

Bo Malmberg

FIGURE 12. RURAL POPULATION GROWTH IN SUB-SAHARAN AFRICA
(MEAN GROWTH RATE 2%)

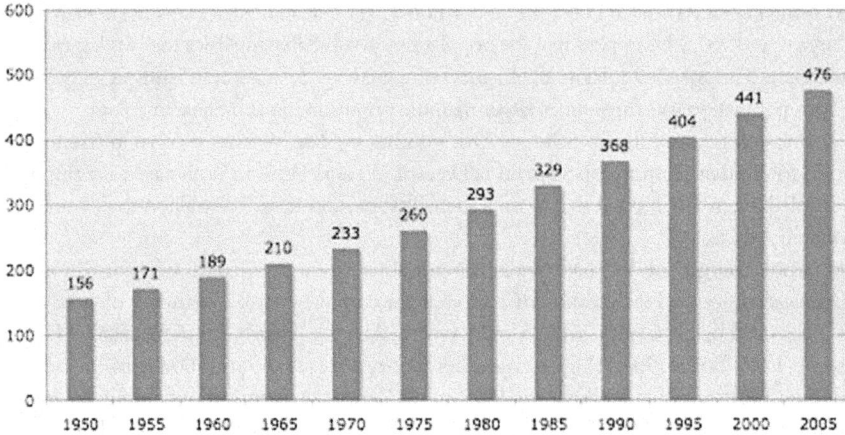

for the urban population. The rural population has tripled between 1950 and 2005, whereas the urban population is 14 times greater than in 1950. At that date, only 20 million people lived in sub-Saharan cities. Today, sub-Saharan Africa has 278 million urban dwellers, and this number has doubled every 15 years since 1950. Sub-Saharan Africa is thus undergoing a veritable urban revolution. The subcontinent has been transformed from a rural hinterland into an increasingly urbanised society.

If sub-Saharan Africa, 40 years from now, has developed into an industrialised region, economic historians will conclude that that basis for this industrialisation was laid during the second half of the 20th century. They will point to the transformation of sub-Saharan agriculture and to the development of an urban sector that was essentially non-existent in 1950. Increasing population pressure on the African countryside and rapid urbanisation have produced much hardship. At the same time, however, there is now an African agricultural sector that is producing four times more than 50 years ago. There also now a large urban labour force and a large informal urban economy. Thus, if sub-Saharan Africa started to expand economically it would not be hard to explain. The question is, if these preconditions for economic growth are in place, why is there not an economic take-off?

7. Age-structure change and economic growth

In a speech given in 1999, Samuel Huntington posed a similar question, and found an answer:

> For decades, economists have grappled with the question, "Why have some countries developed economically and become prosperous, while others remained mired in backwardness and poverty?" They have not been able to find a convincing economic answer. This question struck me with particular force some years ago when I happened to run across economic data on Ghana and South Korea from 1960. At that time, these two countries had almost identical economic profiles in terms of per capita GNP, relative importance of their primary, manufacturing, and service sectors, nature of their exports, and amounts of foreign aid. Thirty years later South Korea had become an industrial giant, with high per capita income, multinational corporations, a major exporter of cars and electronic equipment, while Ghana still remained Ghana. How could one account for this difference in performance? Undoubtedly many factors were responsible, but I became convinced that culture was a large part of the explanation. South Koreans valued thrift, savings, and investment, hard work, discipline, and education. Ghanaians had different values. (*Huntington 1999*).

Huntington thus argued that cultural differences are what determine differences in economic development, and many would be prepared to agree. A problem, however, is that Huntington uses a residual explanation: since the difference cannot be explained by the economic profile, it must be culture. But Huntington hadn't done his homework. During the 1990s it became clear that growth rates in per capita income are strongly affected by changes in the child dependency rate, that is, the ratio between the young non-working age population and the working age population. When the ratio of workers to young non-workers increases, the rate of per capita income growth goes up. And if the young non-working age population grows faster than the working age population, then the per capita income growth rate declines.

Figure 13 shows what has happened to child dependency rate in Korea and Ghana after 1958. In the early 1960s, Ghana and South Korea both had a child dependency rate close to one. This implies that the 0-14 year-old population was almost as large as the 15-64 year-old population. This similarity in demographic structure was mirrored in a similar economic structure, as observed by Huntington. From the mid-1960s, as fertility started to decline rapidly in South Korea, the child dependency rates began to fall and at the same time growth rates in per capita income accelerated. By 2005, the child dependency rate in South Korea approached 0.25. This implies that the working age population is now four times larger than the child population. In Ghana, however, the fertility rate, and hence the child dependency rate, remained high into the 1990s, and Ghana did not experience the explosive growth that characterised South Korea at the time.

What happened in South Korea is not unique to that country. In fact, in all the Asian Tigers, acceleration of per capita income growth has gone hand in hand with large reductions in the child dependency rate. And Ghana is not unique in sub-Saharan Africa. Ninety percent of the Sub-Saharan countries belong to the top-quartile with respect to the child dependency rate. And more than 85% of the countries in the top-quartile are located in sub-Saharan Africa. Thus, today, sub-Saharan Africa has a near monopoly on high child dependency rates.

In the 1960s, however, high dependency rates were a characteristic that sub-Saharan Africa shared with almost all developing countries (see Figure 14). What has happened since 1960 is that fertility rates have declined relatively fast in most other developing countries, whereas

Bo Malmberg

FIGURE 13. CHILD DEPENDENCY RATES IN GHANA AND SOUTH KOREA

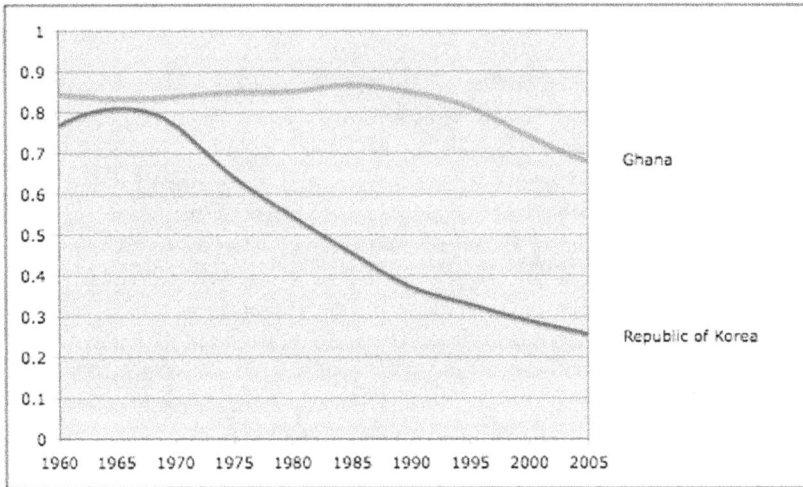

fertility reduction in sub-Saharan Africa has been modest. The effect has been that, today, most of children living in societies with high child dependency rates can be found in sub-Saharan Africa. Moreover, high child dependency rates are a relatively uniform pattern across the sub-continent. Only Botswana and South Africa have child dependency rates below 0.7. All other countries have rates of 0.7 or higher. This is a feature of the current situation that should never be forgotten when the social and economic development of sub-Saharan Africa is discussed.

FIGURE 14. CHILD DEPENDENCY RATE IN A SET OF COUNTRIES/REGIONS (UNITED NATIONS. POPULATION DIVISION 2007)

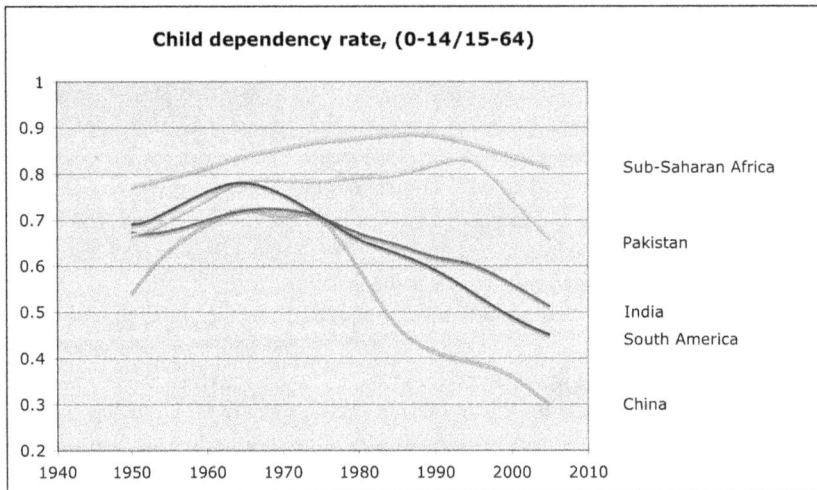

Although the dependency rate has been used as a summary measure of population age structure since the 19th century, it is only more recently that a more systematic exploration of its effect on social and economic development has begun. Interest in the effects of change in dependency rates has been stimulated by the realisation that there are dramatic shifts in the age structure during the demographic transition. This is illustrated in Figure 15 and Figure 16, where changes in the age structure in Kenya and China from 1955 to 2005 are illustrated.

Looking first at Kenya, we see that between 1955 and 1965 population growth was concentrated in the youngest age group, 0-14, primarily because of a decline in under-five mortality.

Between 1965 and 1975, there was continued growth in the 0-14 age group. This is a result of a continued decrease in child mortality, but it is also a reflection of the fact that in this period the 15-29 year age group was growing. That is, the population in fertile ages was expanding and, in a country with high fertility rates, this implies a growing number of childbirths. The increase in the 15-29 age group, in turn, was due to the entry into adult ages of the large 0-14 year cohort from 10-15 years earlier.

FIGURE 15. AGE STRUCTURE CHANGE IN KENYA 1950-2005 (UNITED NATIONS. POPULATION DIVISION 2007)

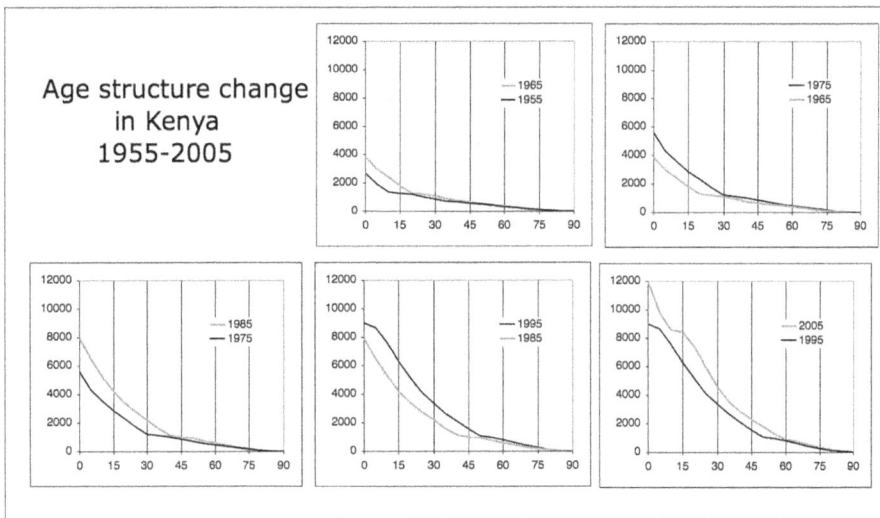

Between 1975 and 1985 there is a continued increase in the 0-14 group that is linked to a continued increase in the fertile adult population and continuing high fertility.

In the next period, 1985-95, there is continuing growth in the adult population and now it is not only the youngest part of the adult population that is growing. There is also growth in the 25-45 age group. At this point, we also see the effect of declining fertility rates on the age structure. Although the fertile adult population continued to expand, there is a slackening in the expansions of the youngest age group. The effect will be a modest reduction in the child dependency ratio.

However, after 1995 fertility reduction has stopped. This has implies that, again, there is rapid growth in the 0-14 group, and also, that there will be no further reductions in the child dependency rate.

Kenya's development can be compared to that of China, shown in Figure 16. We can see that up to 1975, development is in many ways similar. After the sharp post-1975 drop in Chinese fertility, however, there is increasing divergence between the development in China and Kenya. Between 1975 and 1985, population growth in China is concentrated on the youngest part of the working age population. There is very little growth in the 0-14 group.

This is true also for the 1985-95 period, when growth is concentrated to the 20-35 age group, and the 1995-2005 period, when growth is concentrated to the 30-55 age group. The result is that China today has a population that is concentrated on the working ages, with few children and (for another 10-15 years), relatively few older people. The child dependency rate has declined from 0.80 in 1965 to 0.40 today. In Kenya, however, the child dependency rate is still 0.80.

FIGURE 16. AGE STRUCTURE CHANGE IN CHINA 1955-2005 (UNITED NATIONS. POPULATION DIVISION 2007)

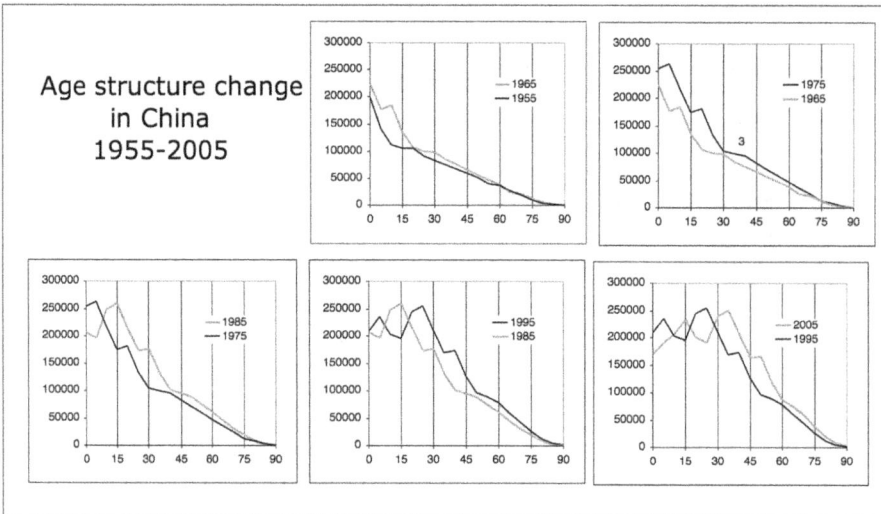

The divergent global trends in the child dependency rates have made it possible for economists to estimate the effect of child dependency on economic development. The results are dramatic. A major part of the difference in per capita income growth between the East Asian Tigers and sub-Saharan Africa can be explained by different trends in the child dependency rate (Bloom, Canning et al. 2000). The effects of changes in the dependency rates on per capita income growth are so strong that David Bloom and his colleges have proposed the term "demographic dividend" for the boost in economic growth that results from the fertility decline (Bloom and Canning 2003). The term dividend is appropriate, since the positive effect on economic growth that results from an improved age structure would not have come about if it were not for the child investment that was made during the high fertility phase of the demographic transition. The dividend concept also underscores the fact that the favourable dependency rate is a transitory phenomenon. Eventually, lower birth rates will result in a growth of the old-age dependency rate and a reduction in the potential for economic growth.

Thus, the short answer to the question why sub-Saharan Africa hasn't entered a phase of rapid economic is that growth in per capita income is held back by high child dependency rates caused by continued high fertility.

High rates of child dependency are very likely a sufficient explanation for low growth rates in per capita income in sub-Saharan Africa. The list of countries with high dependency rates contains no major country that has achieved a high level of economic development. The failure to take into account the strong impact of the child dependency rate is a major shortcoming of the studies on the causes of poor economic performance in sub-Saharan Africa referred to by Bigsten and Durevall (2007).

It is also likely that a reduction in child dependency would dramatically improve the prospects for per capita income growth in sub-Saharan Africa. This is evidenced not only by the development in Eastern Asia, India and many countries in Latin America. The much acclaimed growth acceleration of Ireland has occurred in a period of rapid declines in the child dependency rate, partly the result of making contraception legal in the late 1970s (Bloom and Canning 2003). Reduction in the child dependency rate should also be a positive factor in the acceleration of economic growth in the former socialist countries of Eastern Europe.

Moreover, research on the demographic determinants of economic development has also demonstrated that low mortality is an important precondition for rapid growth in per capita income. If sub-Saharan Africa were to follow the development trajectories of the East Asian growth economies, it would require an ability to reproduce the successful policies for improving population health that were implemented in this region after the Second World War. Improvements in health, in combination with improvements in education, especially for women, are likely to stimulate faster declines in fertility and hence declines in the child dependency rate.

8. Other macroeconomic effects of changing age structure

A potential mechanism behind the effect of age structure on per capita income growth is that declining dependency rates have a positive effect on saving and, hence, on capital accumulation. This hypothesis is also supported by empirical research in the 1990s (Horioka 1991; Kelley and Schmidt 1994; Weil 1994; Kelley and Schmidt 1996; Higgins 1998; Hebertsson and Zoega 1999; Lindh and Malmberg 1999). Age structure's effects on savings had been discussed and demonstrated earlier (Leff 1969; Mason 1987), but they were given renewed attention in the 1990s as a complement to the findings on age effects on economic growth. Sub-Saharan Africa conforms well to this pattern. The child dependency rate is high and savings rates are low (see Bigsten and Durevall 2007)

The savings rate, that is the share of GDP that is not used for consumption, is closely related to the current account or the difference between earnings from exports and payments for imports. If savings are low and the demand for investment in infrastructure, housing and machinery is high, then it will be difficult to find internal sources of finance. In real terms, this implies that the inhabitants of a country are not prepared to abstain from as much consumption as would be necessary to make room for the investments that are required. One solution is, then, to use foreign loans to finance net imports of consumption and investment goods. The need to cut down consumption is then eliminated. Instead, a current account deficit is created that mirrors a low savings rate (Bigsten and Durevall 2007).

Running a current account deficit is, thus, an efficient solution to the problems generated by an increase in the child dependency rate. This can be explained by reference to Figure 17, which presents a stylised version of the economic life cycle. The nearly horizontal line in Figure 17 represents the consumption demand of an individual at different ages. The reason for the horizontality is that there is relatively little change in consumption needs over the life cycle. Infants, children, young adults, prime-aged adults and old individuals require adequate amounts of food, housing, clothing and human care. The productive capacity of individuals, however, changes drastically with age. Zero at birth, it rises as children grow up to reach a maximum somewhere in mid-life, and then declines to approach zero again for those who become old and fragile.

The shape of the consumption and production profile implies that individuals will live through two deficit phases, childhood and old age, when their consumption needs outrun their productive capacity, and one surplus phase when their productive capacity is larger than their consumption needs. In a stable society, the deficits generated by children and old people are balanced by the surplus that working age adults produce. A reduction in infant mortality that increases the number of surviving children will, however, disrupt this balance. Since there is, in the short run, no increase in the size of the working age population, the size of the surplus will be constant. More children, however, imply a larger deficit. Thus, there is no longer a balance between surplus and deficit.

In the national accounts, this can show up as a declining savings rate. One way to accommodate the imbalance could be to reduce investment. Lending from abroad also can solve the problem. This is equivalent to taking advantage of a surplus situation in a different country to solve the deficit situation generated by the increase in child dependency. Thus, as pointed out in a pioneering paper by the Harvard economic historian Jeffrey Williamson, international capital flows can be seen as a form of intergenerational transfer. This idea

FIGURE 17. THE ECONOMIC LIFE CYCLE

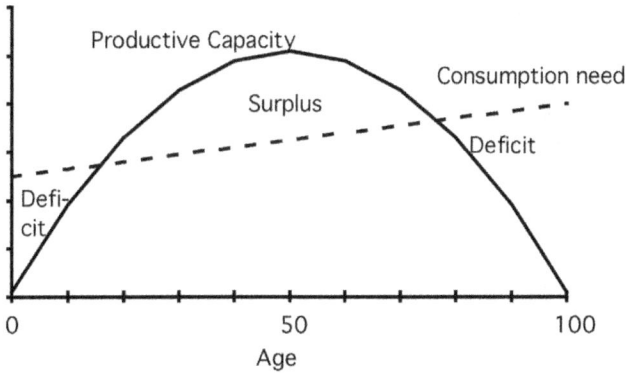

fits very well with the existing data. Countries with high child dependency rates tend to be countries that also run current account deficits, a deficit that turns into a surplus when fertility falls and the child dependency rates decline. The rapid build-up of foreign debt in sub-Saharan Africa after 1970 conforms to this pattern (Bigsten and Durevall 2007).

Current account deficits, though, are not an option for all countries with high child dependency rates. Over time, the debt burden can become overwhelming, especially if the interest rates are high. A further problem is that it takes 15-20 years before a child grows into a working adult that can start to repay the loans taken to finance that child's upbringing. Therefore, other complementary means are needed to accommodate the imbalance created by an increasing child dependency rate. One such solution is development aid. Foreign aid performs a function that is similar to foreign lending but is more adapted to the needs of a country with a high child dependency rate. Just as parents do not expect their children to pay back what their parents have spent on them in their childhood, donors accept that they will receive neither payback nor interest on the funds they have transferred. In accordance with this, sub-Saharan Africa has a high dependency on foreign aid (Bigsten and Durevall 2007)

9. Child labour and poverty

Another means by which the deficit situation can be met is to shift the age-production profile. If children are put to work earlier than before, the extra consumption needs associated with an increasing dependency rate will be easier to meet (Malmberg and Sommestad 2000). The data presented in Figure 18 demonstrate that children indeed start to work earlier in countries where children constitute a large part of the population. In countries where the population share of children below 15 years of age is above 44%, about 30% are of children aged 10-14 are active in the labour force. Of 26 countries in this group, 21 are located in sub-Saharan Africa.

FIGURE 18. CHILD LABOUR AND POPULATION SHARE OF CHILDREN (WORLD BANK 2007)

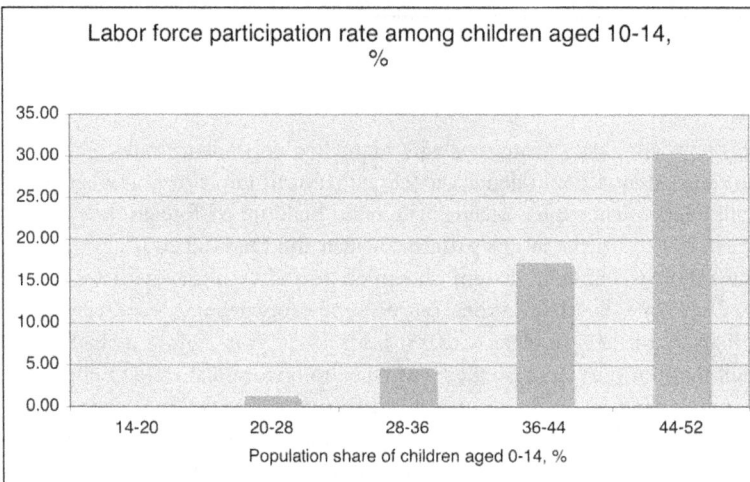

FIGURE 19. POVERTY RATES AND POPULATION SHARE OF CHILDREN (WORLD BANK 2007)

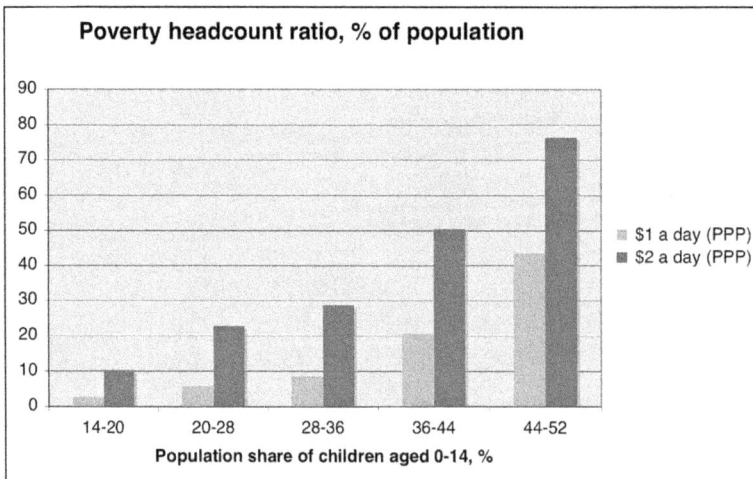

If these attempts to restore the balance between the productive capacity and the consumption needs of a society fail, the result will be that some consumption needs will not be met. In the Millennium Development Goals, the minimum consumption standard has been set at a dollar a day, alternatively two dollars a day. Figure 19 shows how the poverty headcount ratio using these definitions is related to the share of children 0-14 years in the population. Clearly, the risk of being affected by severe poverty is much higher in societies were the share of adults in the population is small. As remarked above, 21 of 26 countries with more than 44% of the population in ages below 15 years are found in sub-Saharan Africa.

10. Migration and social unrest

However, findings on the effects of changing age structure are not restricted to observations on how an increase in the child dependency ratio affects the economy. Another key group is the young adult population. During the demographic transition, the expansion of the young adult population starts some decades after the initial reduction in mortality. What characterises young adulthood is the need to find a livelihood that will enable young people to support themselves and eventually a family. An increase in the number of young adults will, therefore, lead to an increased demand for agricultural land and an increase in the demand for migration to areas where job chances are good. An expansion of the young adult population also constitutes a risk if large groups cannot find a decent livelihood in ordinary employment. It is possible that such situations will make it easier for criminal elements to recruit willing followers. Another possible response, noted already by Malthus, is that young adults react to a more difficult life situation by delaying family formation and child bearing. All these effects of an increasing young adult population have been demonstrated in research presented during the last 15 years. This is highly relevant for sub-Saharan Africa, where the increase in this age group will be very rapid in the next two decades.

With respect to migration, the most extensive work has been done by the English historian Tim Hatton, in collaboration with Jeff Williamson (Hatton, Williamson et al. 1998; Hatton and Williamson 2003). They have demonstrated that surges in migration during the 19th century were linked to rapid growth in the young adult group. They have also applied a similar model to modern data showing that declining fertility in developing countries since 1980 will lead to a decline in the demand for emigration. The exception is sub-Saharan Africa, where continued strong growth in the young adult group will lead to increasing pressures for out-migration. Malmberg (2006) has applied the Hatton-Williamson model to UN data showing that net migration is positively correlated to cohort growth for the 20-24 age group (Malmberg 2006). The size of each cohort was determined by using data on the number of births 20 years earlier and adjusting this number for under-five mortality.

The micro-level foundation for the correlation between the young adult group and migration is that this is the most mobile of all age groups. This was noted by Ravenstein as early as1889 and it is a finding that is replicated in all the studies of the age structure of migrants (Ravenstein 1885). A theoretical explanation for this pattern based on human capital theory was presented by Schwarts in 1976. Her argument is that migration can be seen as an investment and that the return on this investment is higher for individuals with a long remaining work-life (Schwartz 1976).

A demographic explanation for variations in international net migration can be seen as conflicting with the view that migration often has a political background and that many of the international migrant are refugees. This conflict is only apparent though. The reason is that political conflicts, especially of violent nature, have also been shown to be related to increases in the young adult group.

The suggestion that a large youth cohort can introduce social unrest was put forward as far back as 1855 by the Norwegian priest and pioneer sociologist Eilert Sundt. He observed that a large youth cohort stirred labour unrest in Norway in the 1840s (Sundt 1980). Herbert Moller, in 1968, provided an historical overview of the relationship between large youth cohorts and social turbulence (Moller 1968). This theme was developed more extensively by Goldstone (1991).

In his work on ethnic conflicts in Asia, Gary Fuller from the University of Hawaii introduced the concept of youth bulge (Fuller 1995). Fuller used the term to describe a situation where the share of people aged 15-24 years reaches above 20%. The term was popularised by Samuel Huntington's book *The Clash of Civilisations* who, building on Fuller's work, argued that youth bulges in the Arabic world are a major factor behind Muslim resurgence (Huntington 1996). After 9/11, this idea entered into the popular debate and this, in turn, has stimulated serious research into the topic.

An excellent overview of the recent literature is provided by Urdal (2006). In addition, he makes an important contribution to the field by carrying out well-designed tests of the youth bulge hypothesis using a data set on internal armed conflicts from 1950 to 2000. Urdal's conclusion is that the youth bulge hypothesis is correct. As the share of the 15-24 age group in the adult population increases, the risk of internal armed conflict, and also of terrorism and rioting, grows. Urdal discusses different potential explanations for this pattern. One is the *greed* perspective. The explanation here is that a large youth cohort provides a large supply of potential rebel soldiers and that this reduces the cost of recruiting the forces necessary for an attack on the existing government. A second explanation builds on a grievance perspective. Here the idea is that a large youth cohort leads to relative deprivation among young adults and that they, therefore, rebel in order to improve their social position (Urdal 2006).

An innovation in Urdal's study is that he relates the size of the youth cohort to the adult population and not to the total population. According to his estimates, this gives a more clear-cut effect of youth bulges on the risk of internal armed conflict. His argument is that high fertility countries, because of a high child dependency rate, can have a low youth-to-population ratio that does not mirror a low share of young adults in the adult population. In fact, his estimates show that the child-to-youth ratio has a strong and significant positive effect on the risk of internal armed conflict and, moreover, that a high child-to-youth ratio strengthens the effect of high youth-to-population rates on conflict risk.

11. The Future of sub-Saharan Africa: A demographic perspective

Given the correlations between demographic change and social and economic trends, what can be said about the future of sub-Saharan Africa? Our analysis has shown that sub-Saharan Africa is by now *half-way through the demographic transition*. Mortality started to decline in the mid-20th century and since 1980 the total fertility rate has fallen by 25%. But, given the high level when the decline began, fertility is still very high. Sub-Saharan women now, on average, give birth to 5.1 children. This is higher than the fertility rate was in Sweden in the 19th century before the decline started. Sub-Saharan Africa, thus, is still far from reproduction-level fertility.

On the other hand, the current fertility level is close to the total fertility rate in China in the early 1970s and lower than the fertility rate in Iran during the late 1980s. In both these countries the total fertility rate fell from close to or above 5 children per woman to below 3 children per woman in less than 10 years. The UN prediction is that the decline to a total fertility rate below 3 will take 35 years in sub-Saharan Africa, compared to 30 years in India and 25 years in South America.

The UN projects a continuous but relatively slow fertility decline in sub-Saharan Africa. This is consistent with the UN projections for the reduction in infant mortality in the region. In Africa, close to 100 per thousand newborn children do not survive their first year of life. The corresponding figure in India is 50% lower. In South America, China and Iran, it is about 75% lower. Practically no country with an infant mortality rate as high as 100 has experienced a total fertility rate below 3 children per woman in childbearing ages. The UN prediction for sub-Saharan Africa is that the number of infant deaths per thousand newborn will not reach below 50 until after 2040.

The UN projections are based primarily on an extension of current trends. It is possible to consider a development that would be more similar to the Iranian or Chinese experience. However, such a scenario would require a much faster improvement in child health, followed by a steeper decline in fertility of the type observed in countries with rapid declines in infant mortality.

It is too early to tell at what pace sub-Saharan Africa will approach a situation with low fertility and low mortality. The data available, though, suggest that the sub-continent is following the same kind of developing path as other areas, but with a 20-30 year lag. This is both good and less good news.

The good news is that sub-Saharan Africa, eventually, can be expected to experience the acceleration in economic development that is associated with the final phase of the demographic transition: increases in per capita income, reductions in poverty and increasing social stability.

But the promise that the demographic transition, when it has run its course, will lead to a decrease in social ills is of little consolation for those who have to live through the difficult times that characterise much of the second half of the demographic transition. One way to approach the question of what challenges lie ahead for sub-Saharan Africa is to look at development in South America during the 1970s, 1980s and 1990s.

South America is interesting to compare for three reasons. First, this is so because the demographic situation there in the late 1960s was similar to the situation in sub-Saharan Africa today. As can be seen in the table below, there are very close similarities with respect to fertility, infant mortality, child dependency and population growth. Only for life expectancy is there a large difference. Second, according to UN projections, sub-Saharan Africa is also expected to follow demographic trends in the next decades that much resemble the trends seen in South America after 1970. Third, neither in South America nor in sub-Saharan Africa does population density rise to the very high levels one finds in Asia. This makes South America more relevant as a comparison than Asia.

TABLE 1. KEY DEMOGRAPHIC MEASURES FOR SUB-SAHARAN AFRICA AND SOUTH AMERICA
(UNITED NATIONS. POPULATION DIVISION 2007)

	South America 1965-69	Sub-Saharan Africa 2005-09
Infant mortality rate	94.2	93.3
Total fertility rate	5.2	5.1
Child dependency rate	0.77	0.80
Life expectancy at birth	58.5	50.0
Population growth rate	2.47	2.39

Can we expect that the demographic similarities will give rise to social, economic and political trends in sub-Saharan Africa that are close to the trends experienced in South America? In the late 1960s and early 1970s, the development trends in South America were as much discussed as the sub-Saharan Africa situation is today. In spite of the 1960s being declared the "First United Nations Development Decade", few of the South American countries had by the end of the 1960s been able to establish sustained growth rates in per capita income. This pattern continued during the 1970s, 1980s and 1990s, when periods of good growth were interspersed with years of economic troubles. Other economic problems in South America during this period included hyper-inflation, currency crises, large budget deficits and foreign debt defaults.

A major trend in South America in the last three or four decades has been urbanisation. In 1960, almost 50% of the population lived in rural areas. In 2010 this share is expected to be 16%. The result has been an increase in the number of slum dwellers, with more than one-third of the urban population living in slums.

Politically, the years 1970-90 were troublesome, with an increase in the number of military dictatorships, as well as human rights violations and attempts at armed rebellion

It is not unlikely that sub-Saharan Africa in the next 30 years will face the same types of challenge that South American countries have experienced during the past 30 years. With continuing high child dependency rates, it may be as difficult for sub-Saharan Africa to establish a stable positive trend in per capita income as it has been for South America. It may be that the sub-Saharan African countries will be more successful with their economic policies than their South-American counterparts, but it is clear that with a weak economy there are risks of budget deficits, debt-defaults and even bouts of hyper-inflation.

Sub-Saharan Africa has also come closer to being the world's most politically troubled region. Contrary to the trend in other regions in the world, the frequency of armed conflict has been rising in sub-Saharan Africa during the last 15 years. And even if sub-Saharan Africa has become part of the trend towards a reduced number of autocracies, the region is still in arrears with respect to the number of stable democracies.

One positive factor for sub-Saharan Africa today compared to South America 30-40 years ago is the state of the world economy. During the 1970s, the world economy tumbled into an economic crisis with negative effects on the growth rates of most countries. Today, instead, it seems as if the world economy is on track for a period of strong economic expansion. Growth is especially strong in many developing countries in Asia, America and North Africa. If these trends persist, it is possible that the global burden of poverty can be reduced. This would make it possible for the global community to concentrate its efforts on poverty reduction on the continent where the needs are most pressing. Another effect of strong global growth is that the demand for both the natural and human resources of sub-Saharan Africa may increase. Unlike the South American economies that had to struggle in a global environment of sluggish growth, sub-Saharan Africa may be able to profit from these favourable global trends, especially if other regions open up their markets to African exports.

12. Conclusions

Population growth in Africa has laid the foundation for the eventual development of a prosperous region. In 1950, Africa's population was clearly too small for the successful exploitation of her natural resources and agricultural potential. The underdeveloped state of the continent's infrastructure wasn't only a reflection of poverty, it was also a reflection of the sparseness of the population. The problem of under-population was acknowledged by the colonial authorities and some public health measures that were undertaken had the explicit purpose of stimulating population and, in particular, labour force growth.

Since then, sub-Saharan Africa has doubled its population twice, first from 180 million inhabitants in 1950 to 388 million in 1980, and then doubling again to 770 million in 2005. With this increase, sub-Saharan Africa has become one of the most populous regions in the world. Its population is about the same size as the population of North and South America (891 million), Europe (728 million), China (1,315 million) and India (1,103 million). Thus, if sub-Saharan Africa succeeds in taking advantage of its population potential, the subcontinent can become a major player in the world economy.

Today, however, sub-Saharan Africa's share of global GDP is only one-fifth of its population share. The major reason for this is the very high child dependency rate caused by a very high total fertility rate and low life expectancy, based on both high infant mortality and high adult mortality rates.

In global income data sets, no more than 10% of the countries faced with demographic conditions of this type have been able to generate a higher per capita income than 4,000 PPP dollars. Reduced mortality and lower fertility, thus, are central requirements if sub-Saharan Africa is to enter a development trajectory towards increasing per capita incomes and reductions in poverty.

Bibliography

Bigsten, A. and D. Durevall (2007). The African Economy and its Role in the World Economy –A Background Paper to the Swedish Government White Paper on Africa.

Bloom, D.E. and D. Canning (2003). "Contraception and the Celtic Tiger", *Economic and Social Review* 34(3):229–47.

—, et al. (2000). "Population Dynamics and Economic Growth in Asia", *Population and Development Review* 26 (Supplement: Population and Economic Change in East Asia): 257–90.

Boserup, E. (1965). *The Conditions of Agricultural Growth: The Economics of Agrarian Change under Population Pressure*. London: Allen & Unwin.

—, (1981). *Population and Technological Change : A Study of Long-term Trends*. Chicago: University of Chicago Press.

Cain, L. and E. Rotella (2001). "Death and Spending: Urban Mortality and Municipal Expenditure on Sanitation", *Annales de démographie historique* 101(1):139–54.

Davis, K. (1945). "The World Demographic Transition", *Annals of the American Academy of Political and Social Science* 237(Jan):1–11.

Food and Agriculture Organisation of the United Nations (2004). *The State of Food and Agriculture*. Rome: FAO.

Fort, M.P., M.A. Mercer, et al. (2004). *Sickness and Wealth : The Corporate Assault on Global Health*. Cambridge MA: South End Press.

Fuller, G. (1995). "The Demographic Backdrop to Ethnic Conflict: A Geographic Overview", *The challenge of Ethnic Conflict to National and International Order in the 1990s: Geographic Perspectives*. G.R.D. Central Intelligence Agency. [Washington, DC]: Central Intelligence Agency: vi, 194 pp.

Goldstone, J.A. (1991). *Revolution and Rebellion in the Early Modern World*. Berkeley: University of California Press.

Haines, M.R. and R.H. Steckel (2000). *A Population History of North America. Cambridge and New York*: Cambridge University Press.

Hatton, T.J. and J.G. Williamson (2003). "Demographic and Economic Pressure on Emigration Out of Africa", Scandinavian Journal of Economics 105(3):465–86.

—, et al. (1998). *The Age of Mass Migration: Causes and Economic Impact*. New York: Oxford University Press.

Hebertsson, T.T. and G. Zoega (1999). "Trade Surpluses and Life-Cycle Saving Behaviour", *Economics Letters* 65(2):227–37.

Higgins, M. (1998). "Demography, National Savings, and International Capital Flows", *International Economic Review* 39(2):343–69.

Horioka, C.Y. (1991). "The Determinants of Japan's Saving Rate: The Impact of Age Structure of the Population and Other Factors", *Economic Studies Quarterly* 42:237–53.

Huck, P. (1995). "Infant Mortality and Living Standards of English Workers During the Industrial Revolution", *Journal of Economic History* 55(3):528–50.

Huntington, S.P. (1996). *The Clash of Civilizations and the Remaking of World Order*. New York: Simon & Schuster.

—, (1999). "Keynote Address", *Colorado College's 125th Anniversary Symposium, Cultures in the 21st Century: Conflicts and Convergences*, Colorado College.

Kelley, A.C. and R.M. Schmidt (1994). *Population and Income Change: Recent Evidence*. Washington, DC; World Bank.

—, (1996). "Saving, dependency and development", *Journal of Population Economics* 9(4):365–86.

Leff, N.H. (1969). "Dependency Rates and Savings Rates", *American Economic Review* 61: 476–80.

Lindh, T. and B. Malmberg (1999). Age Structure and the Current Account. A Changing Relation? Working Paper Series 1999:21, Department of Economics, Uppsala University.

Malmberg, B. (2006). "The Boom and Bust of Net Migration? A 40-year Forecast", in Palme, J. and K. Tamas (eds), *Globalizing Migration Regimes : New Challenges to Transnational Cooperation*. Aldershot: Ashgate, pp. 36–43.

Malmberg, B. and L. Sommestad (2000). "The Hidden Pulse of History : Age Transition and Economic Change in Sweden, 1820–2000", *Scandinavian Journal of History* 25:130–46.

Mason, A. (1987). "National Savings Rates and Population Growth: A New Model and New Evidence", in Johnson, D.G. and R.D. Lee, *Population Growth and Economic Development: Issues and Evidence*. Madison, University of Wisconsin Press.

Moller, H. (1968). "Youth as a Force in the Modern World", *Comparative Studies in Society and History* 10(3):237–60.

Notestein, F.W. (1945). "Population: The Long View",in Schultz, T.W., *Food for the World*. Chicago: University of Chicago Press, xiv, 352, [1] p.

Ravenstein, E.G. (1885). "The Laws of Migration", *Journal of the Statistical Society of London* 48(2):167–235.

Schwartz, A. (1976). "Migration, Age, and Education", *Journal of Political Economy* 84(4, Part 1):701–20

Sundt, E.L. (1980). *On marriage in Norway*. Cambridge and New York: Cambridge University Press.

United Nations. Population Division (2006). *World Population Prospects : The 2004 Revision*. New York: United Nations.

United Nations. Population Division (2007). *Population Estimates and Projection*, 2006 Revision. New York: United Nations.

Urdal, H. (2006). "A Clash of Generations? Youth Bulges and Political Violence", *International Studies Quarterly* 50:607–29.

Weil, D.N. (1994). "The Saving of the Elderly in Micro and Macro Data", *Quarterly Journal of Economics* 109(1):55–81.

World Bank (2007). *World Development Indicators Online*, World Bank Group.

CURRENT AFRICAN ISSUES PUBLISHED BY THE INSTITUTE
Recent issues in the series are available electronically
for download free of charge www.nai.uu.se

1. *South Africa, the West and the Frontline States. Report from a Seminar.* 1981, 34 pp, (out-of print)

2. Maja Naur, *Social and Organisational Change in Libya.* 1982, 33 pp, (out-of print)

3. *Peasants and Agricultural Production in Africa. A Nordic Research Seminar. Follow-up Reports and Discussions.* 1981, 34 pp, (out-of print)

4. Ray Bush & S. Kibble, *Destabilisation in Southern Africa, an Overview.* 1985, 48 pp, (out-of print)

5. Bertil Egerö, *Mozambique and the Southern African Struggle for Liberation.* 1985, 29 pp, (out-of print)

6. Carol B.Thompson, *Regional Economic Polic under Crisis Condition. Southern African Development.* 1986, 34 pp, (out-of print)

7. Inge Tvedten, *The War in Angola, Internal Conditions for Peace and Recovery.* 1989, 14 pp, (out-of print)

8. Patrick Wilmot, *Nigeria's Southern Africa Policy 1960–1988.* 1989, 15 pp, (out-of print)

9. Jonathan Baker, *Perestroika for Ethiopia: In Search of the End of the Rainbow?* 1990, 21 pp, (out-of print)

10. Horace Campbell, *The Siege of Cuito Cuanavale.* 1990, 35 pp, (out-of print)

11. Maria Bongartz, *The Civil War in Somalia. Its genesis and dynamics.* 1991, 26 pp, (out-of print)

12. Shadrack B.O. Gutto, *Human and People's Rights in Africa. Myths, Realities and Prospects.* 1991, 26 pp, (out-of print)

13. Said Chikhi, Algeria. *From Mass Rebellion to Workers' Protest.* 1991, 23 pp, (out-of print)

14. Bertil Odén, *Namibia's Economic Links to South Africa.* 1991, 43 pp, (out-of print)

15. Cervenka Zdenek, *African National Congress Meets Eastern Europe. A Dialogue on Common Experiences.* 1992, 49 pp, ISBN 91-7106-337-4, (out-of print)

16. Diallo Garba, *Mauritania–The Other Apartheid?* 1993, 75 pp, ISBN 91-7106-339-0, (out-of print)

17. Zdenek Cervenka and Colin Legum, *Can National Dialogue Break the Power of Terror in Burundi?* 1994, 30 pp, ISBN 91-7106-353-6, (out-of print)

18. Erik Nordberg and Uno Winblad, *Urban Environmental Health and Hygiene in Sub-Saharan Africa.* 1994, 26 pp, ISBN 91-7106-364-1, (out-of print)

19. Chris Dunton and Mai Palmberg, *Human Rights and Homosexuality in Southern Africa.* 1996, 48 pp, ISBN 91-7106-402-8, (out-of print)

20. Georges Nzongola-Ntalaja *From Zaire to the Democratic Republic of the Congo.* 1998, 18 pp, ISBN 91-7106-424-9, (out-of print)

21. Filip Reyntjens, *Talking or Fighting? Political Evolution in Rwanda and Burundi, 1998–1999.* 1999, 27 pp, ISBN 91-7106-454-0, SEK 80.-

22. Herbert Weiss, *War and Peace in the Democratic Republic of the Congo.* 1999, 28 pp, ISBN 91-7106-458-3, SEK 80,-

23. Filip Reyntjens, *Small States in an Unstable Region – Rwanda and Burundi, 1999–2000,* 2000, 24 pp, ISBN 91-7106-463-X, (out-of print)

24. Filip Reyntjens, *Again at the Crossroads: Rwanda and Burundi, 2000–2001.* 2001, 25 pp, ISBN 91-7106-483-4, (out-of print)

25. Henning Melber, *The New African Initiative and the African Union. A Preliminary Assessment and Documentation.* 2001, 36 pp, ISBN 91-7106-486-9, (out-of print)

26. Dahilon Yassin Mohamoda, *Nile Basin Cooperation. A Review of the Literature.* 2003, 39 pp, ISBN 91-7106-512-1, SEK 90,-

27. Henning Melber (ed.), *Media, Public Discourse and Political Contestation in Zimbabwe.* 2004, 39 pp, ISBN 91-7106-534-2, SEK 90,-

28. Georges Nzongola-Ntalaja, *From Zaire to the Democratic Republic of the Congo.* Second and Revised Edition. 2004, 23 pp, ISBN-91-7106-538-5, (out-of print)

29. Henning Melber (ed.), *Trade, Development, Cooperation – What Future for Africa?* 2005, 44 pp, ISBN 91-7106-544-X, SEK 90,-

30. Kaniye S.A. Ebeku, *The Succession of Faure Gnassingbe to the Togolese Presidency – An International Law Perspective.* 2005, 32 pp, ISBN 91-7106-554-7, SEK 90,-

31. Jeffrey V. Lazarus, Catrine Christiansen, Lise Rosendal Østergaard, Lisa Ann Richey, *Models for Life – Advancing antiretroviral therapy in sub-Saharan Africa.* 2005, 33 pp, ISBN 91-7106-556-3, SEK 90,-

32. Charles Manga Fombad and Zein Kebonang, *AU, NEPAD and the APRM – Democratisation Efforts Explored.* Edited by Henning Melber. 2006, 56 pp, ISBN 91-7106-569-5, SEK 90,-

33. Pedro Pinto Leite, Claes Olsson, Magnus Schöldtz, Toby Shelley, Pål Wrange, Hans Corell and Karin Scheele, *The Western Sahara Conflict – The Role of Natural Resources in Decolonization.* Edited by Claes Olsson. 2006, 32 pp, ISBN 91-7106-571-7, SEK 90,-

34. Jassey, Katja and Stella Nyanzi, *How to Be a "Proper" Woman in the Times of HIV and AIDS.* 2007, 35 pp, ISBN 91-7106-574-1, SEK 90,-

35. Lee, Margaret, Henning Melber, Sanusha Naidu and Ian Taylor, *China in Africa.* Compiled by Henning Melber. 2007, 47 pp, ISBN 978-91-7106-589-6, SEK 90,-

36. Nathaniel King, *Conflict as Integration. Youth Aspiration to Personhood in the Teleology of Sierra Leone's 'Senseless War'.* 2007, 32 pp, ISBN 978-91-7106-604-6, SEK 90,-

37. Aderanti Adepoju, *Migration in sub-Saharan Africa.* 2008. 70 pp, ISBN 978-91-7106-620-6 SEK 90,-

38. Bo Malmberg, *Demography and the development potential of sub-Saharan Africa.* 2008, 39 pp, 978-91-7106-621-3, SEK 90,-